FONTANA
POCKET LIBRARY OF GREAT ART

Plate 1. VLAMINCK, PAINTING *Photo Karquel*

MAURICE DE

VLAMINCK

(1876 - 1958.)

text by

ROBERT REY

COLLINS
Fontana Pocket Library of Great Art

On the cover
BICYCLE RACE AT VERNEUIL
Collection Roudinesco
31⅞ x 24¾"

Plate 2. VALMONDOIS. *c. 1925. Lithograph*
Bibliothèque nationale, Paris

More than any other painter, Maurice de Vlaminck, the man, is of a piece with the works he created. The very name evokes the metallic sound of a hammer striking an anvil; by merely pronouncing it we are transported to Flanders, land of De Connink and Philippe d'Artevelde. It is to them that Vlaminck owes his congenital need of independence. An anti-conformist before birth, he will remain anti-conformist after death.

Plate 3. REGION OF L'ISLE-ADAM. *1923. Etching and engraving.*
Bibliothèque nationale

This complete aloofness from conventions, whether those of middle-class life or of Bohemia, in his case results not so much from aggressiveness as from an instinctive reserve. In the presence of certain aspects of nature, Vlaminck's emotion and wonder burst forth irresistibly on the canvas. If he tried to hold them back, to filter, control, "expound" them, they would grow cold and wither away. They would lose their brilliance like those fish whose iridescence dies with them.

This liberating projection, however, is something that takes place primarily between him and his painting. He would not relish being caught in the act of transference. For all that he is a big hulk of a man, Vlaminck is rather shy. No wonder that he shuns human company, at least the company of those who would be so glad to lionize him because of his fame.

For he feels at home with a very different kind of people, people whose tastes and inclinations are as

Plate 4. RUE DE LA GLACIÈRE. *1920. Etching and engraving*
Bibliothèque nationale

vigorous and simple as his own: between them and him
there is a continual exchange of joy and strength. As
a child, in his grandfather's café at Wambrechies, and
as an adolescent competing with bicycle racers and, like
them, straining on the high gear bikes (or pulling the
oar with all his strength at the Chatou regattas),
Vlaminck had the kind of security he has always needed.

Today, burdened though not bent by the years, he lives withdrawn in the depth of the countryside in Perche.

As a result of mutations whose secret will probably never be fathomed, some men who are of "common" stock develop specifically "noble" needs and aptitudes. I think that Vlaminck is a case in point.

His father, who began as a humble tailor, became a musician so capable that he presently supported himself not by his needle but by his violin.

His mother was an obscure but accomplished pianist. And as a kind of young Ingres, it was by playing the violin that Maurice earned his and his first wife's bread, and soon that of the three children born of this first marriage — Solange, Yolande, and a third daughter whose recent death caused him great sorrow.

Maurice de Vlaminck, son of Flanders, was born in Paris, Rue Pierre-Lescot, on April 4, 1876.

His early years were spent in the unlikely surroundings of Le Vésinet, a suburb beloved by the wealthy bourgeois of the Third Republic. At the elementary school of Le Vésinet he was a lamentable pupil: he painted there. Already! From a harness-maker who painted in the intervals between making saddles came the revelation of art. Soon, in addition to music for which he had an innate sense, and to painting which enchanted him, Vlaminck became interested in bicycles. This machine, still a novelty, introduced him to the exhilaration of triumph. For some time Vlaminck was a "professional," as we say today.

What was he going to become in the end? Teacher of violin? or of billiards (he was an expert player)? swimming instructor? bicycle racer? painter?

While waiting for this question to be settled he became a soldier, which gave him time to make up his

Plate 5. MARIE. *Woodcut*

mind. The World's Fair of 1900 opened as he left the service; Maurice de Vlaminck went back to his violin. In night clubs, little theaters, and beer gardens he langorously played *valses lentes.*

Somewhere between Paris and Chatou, Vlaminck met Derain. As a matter of fact they did not belong to the same social class, for Derain was the son of a

Plate 6. VALMONDOIS. *1924. Lithograph. Bibliothèque nationale*

dairyman and ice cream confectioner, licensed merchant at Chatou — almost a "gentleman." However, the same rebellions were brewing in both, and then Derain too painted. They became close friends, and this resulted in the birth of Fauvism.

Is it possible to see in Gauguin and in the Nabis (at their beginnings) something like the dawn of Fauvism. (What I have in mind is Gauguin's so-called "synthetism," as Serusier explained it in 1888 in the course of a revealing conversation that Maurice Denis recorded in his famous article in *L'Occident*.) But this was not the case; it was rather a kind of coincidence. Gauguin and his companions, in their Breton solitude, were saturated with intellectualism. They advocated a very ancient conception of painting, which however had so completely fallen into oblivion that they appeared to have invented it; and they backed it up with rules and theories. Fauvism was the very opposite of this: beginning with the duo Vlaminck-Derain it negated all laws,

Plate 7. VALMONDOIS. *1924. Etching and engraving*
Bibliothèque nationale

took exception to all theories. The two leading Fauves
were bent on expressing only spontaneous impulse and
rebelliousness. Down with shades and nuances, the realm
of people with refined tastes, with "good manners":
they set out to be "ill-mannered." André Salmon once

Plate 8. CHURCH OF LE BEAUCHE IN LE PERCHE. *1938.*
Etching and engraving. Bibliothèque nationale

said that Vlaminck "showed off his unculture." This was meant to be clever.

This "unculture" was incidentally all pretense, for Vlaminck had read and written a great deal. Even today he paints and writes more vigorously than ever. His sentences are pithy, full of imagery; he has the rare gift of the right word; he easily ranges from satire to the most incandescent fantasy. Impelled by an insatiable demon, Vlaminck cannot help painting and writing.

Vlaminck perceives the outside world with an extraordinary vehemence. In each tree, in each hovel, in each fruit, he anticipates a life whose discovery fills him with an inexhaustible and almost sacred wonder.

To resort to deliberate distortions in representing the world, to alter the volumes, to break them up only in

Plate 9. L'ISLE-ADAM. *1925. Lithograph*

order to rebuilt monstrous images with the fragments
— that is, in Vlaminck's eyes, the most satanic of crimes.

On this score, he hated and still hates Cubism.
Even before August 1914 Vlaminck had sensed the
hideous face of war in the first Cubist canvases. The
supporters of abstract art would thus be ill-advised to
tell him that the earth is a repertory that has been worn
threadbare as a result of forty thousand years of
"representationalism," and that nothing new can be
discovered in it.

Before a painting by Vlaminck we become aware
of the utter falseness of the French word for "still life"
— *nature morte.*

How could we maintain that a side of beef painted
by him is a fragment of a corpse? In the first place, it

Plate 10. AFTER THE HARVEST IN LE PERCHE. *1948. Drawing*

requires time for a dead creature, whether it be a man or an animal, to become a corpse. Again, this red and clean meat, this fat that will sizzle on the fire and be transformed into a fragrance pleasing to the gods (as can be seen in Homer), brimming over with a fluid ready to take on another life in our own greedy entrails. The fowl bled white, so tragic with its hanging neck and stiff legs will once more be throbbing blood and flesh by means of our bodily alchemy. Even the fish, in their glistening rigidity, remind us of some stories from the Scriptures, of Tobias, of the miraculous draught of fishes, as though Vlaminck were proclaiming the cruel and sovereign right that God is said to have given to man, the right to use everything for his nourishment in order to make nature's splendors an integral part of himself.

Under Vlaminck's eyes, the countryside in autumn enters a triumphant agony. The imminent end makes its colors flare up. The trees display their branches as if

Plate 11. VILLAGE CAFÉ. *1950. Drawing*

they were arms, as if the executioner had begun to strip
them, as they twist in rebellion. When the soil regur-
gitates the water that drenches it, this water reflects the
trees as figures of despair.

Vlaminck participates in the life of the countryside, in the life of the river as well as in the life of the
sea. For he knows that a wave is not *one* thing, and
that the flat, slightly oily water on which his racing
scull once glided between Le Pecq and Chatou, will, on
reaching the end of its course, become that infinite
repertory of temptation and treachery which is the sea.
Another painter, to whom Vlaminck is akin — Courbet
— saw this also, and painted it. But to Courbet the sea
is not an object for contemplation. Before the breakers
whose foamy fury he lays on with a full brush, he
maintains the self-assurance of the tamer in the lion cage.
Vlaminck, who is closer to the gods, is not so presumpt-
uous. With long dragging strokes he follows the surge

Plate 12. ROAD NEAR VALMONDOIS. *Drawing*

of the choppy sea as, wave after wave, cruelly tossing the poor ships beyond the jetty, it pours into the inner harbor and grows calmer.

Even though the sea does not occupy a major place in his works I mention it here because the few canvases inspired by it clearly show the elements of Vlaminck's poetry — a religious love of nature, which he admires and fears; a pantheism, no doubt unconscious, but of a burning fervor; and an animist view of all things.

If Vlaminck, walking on some road of the Beauce with beautiful vistas at the end of a summer's day, heard, as once did the pilot Thamas, a mighty voice raised in mourning, crying, "Pan, the Great Pan is Dead," I am sure he would shout into the wind, "It isn't true!"

Plate 14. ROAD NEAR AUVERS. 1925. *Lithograp*
Bibliothèque nationale

Plate 13. NESLES-LA-VALLÉE. *1925. Lithograph*
Bibliothèque nationale

Plate 15. ONE OF VLAMINCK'S DAUGHTERS. *Drawing*
Bibliothèque nationale

Plate 16. RUEIL-LA-GADELIÈRE. *1955. Drawing*

VLAMINCK SPEAKS...

"After all that has been written about art, Art
with a capital A, I don't like to speak about art."
From *Paysages et personnages*

"Pure painting? Color straight from the tube? These
elementary means that I used instinctively fifty
years ago have become slogans and intellectual
theories! . . . . In the orchestra I conducted, I decided,
in order to make myself heard, to use only brasses,
cymbals, and the bass drum, which in this case were
tubes of color. Just as I would have ordered my
musicians to blow with all their strength into their
saxophones, cornets, and slide-trombones, so I

squeezed tubes of paint onto my canvas, and used only vermilions, chromes, greens, and Prussian blues to scream what I wanted to say."

Ibid.

"In the face of tableaux composed by nature, tableaux that vanish the moment they are born to be re-composed in a different form — in the face of this spectacle, our feelings, our reminiscences, our memories, our forgotten emotions, intransmissible and fugitive, are called forth, are born, and evaporate, leaving behind the certainty that we shall never experience them again — vibrations that are sympathetically echoed by the strings of a harp hidden in our subconscious, in the depth of our being, in our soul and in our heart.

All my life I have tried to paint those feelings which cannot be translated into spoken or written words. I have used colors to stop the moving reel of time, to fix it on the canvas. I have tried to re-create in the beholder emotions that were believed to be buried and gone forever by making use as props of other landscapes, other subjects, other objects."

Ibid.

"What I wanted to paint was the object itself, with its weight and density, as though I were representing it in the very material of which it was formed. My purpose was to show the inner, real life of the object, its essential being in relation with the emotion it released in me."

Ibid.

"Painting is not one of those pleasant occupations which can be counted on as a means of support."

From *Portraits avant décès*

COLOUR PLATES

The commentaries that follow are not conceived in a spirit of aestheticism.

They are confined to a record of the recollections, technical remarks, and other thoughts that occurred to Vlaminck when, in the company of this writer, he looked over the pictures that were chosen for reproduction in this book.

PLATE 17

Painted 1900

PÈRE BOUJU

29⅛ x 19¼"

This portrait, so hastily sketched with a few power-ful strokes of roughly mixed paint, represents a nondescript character who called himself a worker. His exact occupation was unknown: sometimes he said he was a docker, and sometimes a Seine river fisherman.

He often came to the studio occupied by Vlaminck and Derain at Chatou, and bored them with his insipid chatter. To silence this intruder for moment, and to take advantage of his presence, Vlaminck one day used him as the model for this vigorous and caricatural effigy, in which we sense the artist's exasperation with Père Bouju's tall stories.

PLATE 18

Painted 1906

THE DANCER AT THE "RAT MORT"

Collection A. Fried

28¾ x 25¼"

In the early period of Fauvism when it was as brilliant as a freshly opened cactus flower, Derain, Dufy, and Vlaminck strove for violent combinations of color; they also sought to combine color and emotion, for this art, far from being "abstract", aims at explicit syntheses which fuse together sensations of all kinds experienced by the artist. Among the keenest of these sensations are those produced by the contact between an individual's state of mind and the quality of his surroundings.

This night club *entraineuse* is shown at work — a type of work that consists primarily of waiting. While she is tense and serious, she is paradoxically placed in surroundings that hold the promise of gaiety, insouciance, and voluptuousness.

Such is the secret drama that Vlaminck exposed in canvases like this one, in which the vehemence of the palette tragically emphasizes the weariness of the subject lying in wait for customers.

Plate 19. HOUSE IN THE WOODS

(commentary follows color plate section)

Plate 20. CANDLESTICK AND FRUIT STAND

(commentary follows color plate section)

PLATE 21

Painted 1922

SELF-PORTRAIT

21⅝ x 15"

Vlaminck painted this portrait at Valmondois, standing before a mirror. He later repeated this attempt two or three times. The rugged sincerity of his talent is apparent here. The fixed stare imposes an unusual degree of immobility on the model. This picture shows Vlaminck as he was toward his fortieth year—massive, cylindrical, with his crumpled hat serving as an extension of this face inscribed between two severely parallel straight lines, as if it were the outline of a tower. He wears no necktie. This ornamental article of haberdashery, which originated as part of the uniform worn under Louis XV by the regiment of the "Royal Croatians" (hence the French word *cravate*), Vlaminck looks upon as the most ridiculous of all articles of clothing. But he does wear a scarf. Vlaminck has always refused to wear anything but scarves — and such scarves!

Plate 22. WHEAT FIELD OF THE BEAUCE

(commentary follows color plate section)

PLATE 23

Painted 1905

PICNIC

Collection L. Bourdon

Vlaminck painted this picture in the woods near Bougival, in the spring. The figures represented are his brother and his sister-in-law Marguerite.

Although he was an admirer of Manet and of his famous *Luncheon on the Grass* which was painted indoors, and is full of allusions, Vlaminck, then at the height of his Fauvist period, wanted on the contrary to fix on canvas only the visual impact of this couple against the mottled background of sunlit foliage and the luxuriant vegetation of springtime.

(commentary follows color plate section)

PLATE 23

Painted 1905

PICNIC

Collection L. Bourdon

Vlaminck painted this picture in the woods near Bougival, in the spring. The figures represented are his brother and his sister-in-law Marguerite.

Although he was an admirer of Manet and of his famous *Luncheon on the Grass* which was painted indoors, and is full of allusions, Vlaminck, then at the height of his Fauvist period, wanted on the contrary to fix on canvas only the visual impact of this couple against the mottled background of sunlit foliage and the luxuriant vegetation of springtime.

PLATE 24

Painted 1907

CHATOU, VIEW FROM
THE LEFT BANK OF THE SEINE

Museum of Modern Art, Paris

25⅝ x 31½"

This canvas is particularly characteristic of what is called Fauvism. It is one of the group of paintings produced by Vlaminck and Derain in their Chatou studio, which had formerly been occupied by the Le Vanneux restaurant. They inspired several young painters, and they are referred to as the works of the "School of Chatou." Chatou became a Fauvist center.

At that time Vlaminck usually reduced his motifs to a few essential elements and a few very vivid and violently clashing colors. This method of "synthesizing" his vision into a small number of forms and colorations has some analogies with Gauguin's "synthetism" of 1890. But with this fundamental difference, that whereas for Gauguin and his emulators synthetism was an intellectual doctrine, the Fauves wanted merely to upset the conventions so dear to the public.

PLATE 25

SALVIA

One day Godelieve, Vlaminck's little daughter, playfully arranged this small bouquet of salvia and wild roses. Her father recorded its exuberance, capturing it on the wing, as it were. He renders the hollows of the rose petals by a turning motion of his thumb in the fresh paint. Such a picture is better painted with one's fingers than with the brush.

Seen under a magnifying glass it would provide us, I think, with an amazing collection of the painter's fingerprints.

PLATE 26

Painted 1907

LONGCHAMP PADDOCK

Collection L. Bourdon

Here we are still in full Fauvism. Vlaminck has never felt at ease in the world of fashionable society, whose formalities tire his nature, prone to blunt expansiveness. The reason he sometimes visited race courses was that the flicker of colors, the clashing and swirling of forms in motion provided him with an opportunity for those mixtures of pure colors which fill him with an almost physical pleasure. But he found such opportunities more often and in a more lively, more "popular" atmosphere at the Vélodrôme d'Hiver, which had witnessed his own exploits as a bicycle racer.

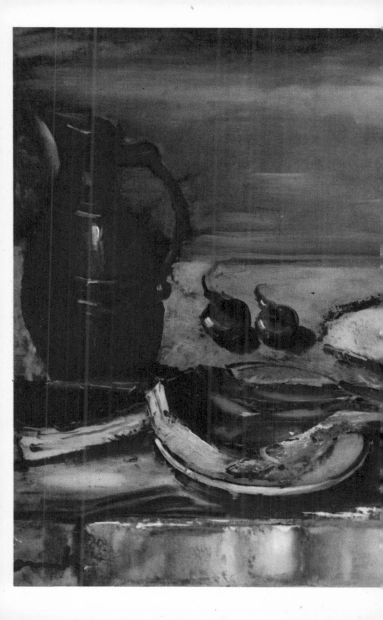

PLATE 27

Painted 1928

FRUITS OF THE EARTH

To Vlaminck, food has a kind of
sacred aspect. He does not analyze
his sensations, nor his methods of
giving them plastic expression. He
communicates them to us im-
periously, as he himself experienced them. For Chardin, the interest-
ing thing about a loaf of bread,
a quarter of meat, a dish laden
with fruit, or two onions on a
sturdy pinewood table is only the
beauty of forms and the richness
or delicacy of colors; whereas in
Vlaminck such objects also arouse
deep feelings. The aspect he gives
them results from his knowledge,
based on experience, of the accu-
mulated efforts thanks to which
they exist and have become what
they are. He knows them also as
the sustenance of life.

Plate 28. HARVEST IN A STORM

(commentary follows color plate section)

PLATE 29

Painted 1932

FISHING BOAT

Collection Roudinesco

25⅜ x 36¼"

An authentic poet, Vlaminck inevitably has an entirely animistic conception of the sea. For him it is far more than an entity — indeed, more than an allegory. As against its immensity he considers himself tiny — though not so tiny as to remain unnoticed. The dangerous changeability of the sea attracts him like an evil spell. It was not until 1939, at Granville, that he stressed the calming quality of the sea at this place, under a sky saturated with vapor whose iridescence is reflected by the sands rather than by the water.

Vlaminck tells us about it in his own words: "I prefer the plains to the sea, I am a landlubber rather than a sailor. The sight of the sea plunges me into deep anxiety. The sea frightens me; before it I feel weak, frail, helpless. Its perfidious and hypocritical calm does not deceive me, it seems to conceal the jealousy and hostility that that the sea has for me."

PLATE 30

Painted 1937

STILL LIFE WITH BREAD

23⅝ x 31⅞"

Vlaminck painted this still life two years after he had settled at La Tourillière.

To eat is to perform a religious rite. Sensitive persons such as Vlaminck here instinctively detect the mystery by virtue of which the outside world is integrated into a human being. This is the meaning of Communion: the broken bread, the poured wine; eat, this is my body, drink, this is my blood....

In this painting which is so solemn, everything expresses both power and humility. The thick glass asks to be lifted carefully, with one's whole hand. The bottle holding the wine is a tower; the knife, the ordinary table knife which will cut these fruits becomes quite naturally an attribute of a sacrificial priest.

Plate 31. ROAD FROM ALENCON TO LE MANS

(commentary follows color plate section)

PLATE 32

Painted 1951

APPROACH TO LA TOURILLIÈRE

21¼ x 28¾"

This is one of the farms belonging to Vlaminck. He bought it in 1937; it is called "Haute Folie". Wheat fields, a few fruit trees, farm buildings — the whole is firmly rooted in the soil, under a limitless sky.

This is the land which Vlaminck sees on waking. He needs to know that his eyes rest on *his* land, that no one is trying to encroach upon it: his nature includes a considerable degree of mistrust.

PLATE 33

Painted 1947

STILL LIFE WITH WHISKY

21¼ x 28¾"

Vlaminck painted this still life in the dining room at La Tourillière. It shows to what extent he is sensitive to the fullness of forms. Scornful of the artifices of Cubism, he organizes the symphony of spheres, ovoids, and cylinders which are, plastically speaking, the framework of objects. Between a pitcher held by a peasant in a painting by Louis Le Nain and the stoneware pot presiding over this conclave of everyday objects, there is a difference in style but not in feeling.

Everything in Vlaminck is related to sincerely experienced sensations. If he records in large letters a label on a bottle, it is because the arrangement of these letters has something to do with the wish the painter had that day to paint this still life rather than any other.

"I never drink anything," says Vlaminck, "except water and whisky — barrels of water for every two fingers of whisky; if it were the other way round, I'd be dead long ago." Note this: It is no accident that *Nana* is included in this painting. "What I like in Zola is his wild romanticism," says Vlaminck. "Without it Zola would be 'undrinkable'."

Plate 34. THE BOISSY-MAUGIS ROAD IN LE PERCHE

(commentary follows color plate section)

PLATE 35

Painted 1947

A BUNCH OF FLOWERS

25 ⅝ x 21¼"

Nothing is less artistically "decadent" than the art
of Vlaminck. It is at the opposite pole to Des
Esseintes, Huysmans' hero so naive in his sophistica-
tion. Nevertheless Vlaminck is not insensitive to the
slightly morbid charm that is exhaled by flowers
when they begin to fade. Possibly a tender melan-
choly impels him to paint once again this or that
bunch before its many withered splendors end up in
the rubbish. At La Tourillière, Godelieve is in charge
of the flowers. The bunch shown here combines, pell-
mell, roses, poppies, anemones, marigolds, and daisies
of the kind called in France "ostrich feathers". Their
curled up petals burst forth from the vase, enhancing
the impression of abundance conveyed by the mottled
colors of this picture.

Plate 36. ARCOTTE, ON THE ORLEANS ROAD

(commentary follows color plate section)

Painted 1908

HOUSE IN THE WOODS

Museum of Modern Art, Paris

20½ x 28⅜"

We are still at the birthplace of Fauvism. The valley of the Seine beyond Paris provided river and farm landscapes, and in painting them the Fauves directly succeeded their elders — Seurat with his *Grande Jatte,* Renoir with his boating parties, and Caillebotte, president of the Nautical Club of the Lower Seine, not to mention the heroes of literature who had preceded them — the Goncourt brothers, with their *Manette Salomon.* The site shown here is in the hills near Bougival, at the center of a cross-roads whose various arms lead to Carrières-St-Denis, Le Pecq, Bezons, Argenteuil, and finally, and particularly, to the *île fleurie* of Nanterre and the inn of Père Fournaise. There, in summer, in the tangle of grass, the ground sloped down to the river banks covered with softly crumbling moss.

Painted c. 1913

CANDLESTICK AND FRUIT STAND

Collection Mr. and Mrs. Harry N. Abrams, New York

24 x 29"

Seemingly inanimate objects come to life when there are no people around.

Looking through a keyhole into a closed and silent room, at a corner of a table laden with household utensils, we have the impression that they are quite different from what we thought they were, and that they are engaged in a kind of conversation. Vlaminck does not have to peep through a keyhole to sense such relationships. Intensely receptive, keenly primitive, he does not intimidate objects by his presence. And they obscurely sense a kinship with him, particularly those objects which, because the material of which they are made is robust, and because the uses to which they are put are simple, — objects like this stoneware pot, thin earthenware fruit stand with real fruit, this candlestick.

Painted 1928

WHEAT FIELDS OF THE BEAUCE

Collection Roudinesco

31⅞ x 39⅝″

Painted by Vlaminck shortly after he settled at La Tourillière, this canvas with its immense wheat fields swaying in the wind like a golden tide under an immense sky, is a good image of Vlaminck's most constant desires and intimate thoughts. His vitality is kindled before the vitality of this wheat springing from the ground as though driven by an irresistible force. "The sight of a wheat field always moves me deeply," he says in one of his books. He feels apprehensive when a gust of wind bends the stalks, and threatens to flatten them to the ground. His own productivity (Delacroix noted that productivity is in itself a characteristic of great creators) is stimulated by these inexhaustible energies. The little church of Lauvilliers-les-Perche with its vertical steeple stands quietly amidst the swirling forms. The endless horizons of the Beauce flatlands have attracted the air force, which established a camp in this part of the country, near Brézolles, taking 1,200 hectares from the ocean of wheat. Vlaminck is unhappy about this.

Painted 1945

HARVEST IN A STORM

23⅝ x 28¾"

As we have seen, for Vlaminck a grain field is not merely a motif, but an extension of his own sensibility.

A secret, all-consuming attraction occurs between the stalks of grain and the painter, with alternations of tenderness and violence. He knows where the wheat comes from, what alchemy transforms the fertilizer it requires into a golden organ with millions of voices; he knows the breezes that make it undulate like a yellow cat bending its back under a caress, the storms that beat it down, the rains that drench it, the sacrificial gesture of the scythe or of the reaping machine that severs it from the earth and heaps it up in loose sheaves, which, after being aligned, look like an army of bearded soldiers.

Vlaminck's own flesh and blood — his daughter Edwige — presides over the sowing, the fertilizing, the culture, the harvest. She is deputy mayor of Rueil. The wheat grown here is not the hard or macaroni variety cultivated in Russia and in Italy, but a species that yields a great amount of flour, which is made into large quantities of bread. When Vlaminck paints wheat, it is as though he were eating of this bread.

Painted 1953

ROAD FROM ALENÇON TO LE MANS

23⅝ x 28¾"

Vlaminck finds his surprises and emotions in nature alone. Today man does not see in a landscape what he would have seen in it at the time of Corot, that is to say, trails, undergrowth, bridle paths. Today man sees only the landscape enframed in his windshield, while his car devours the road — the road with its tones of gray velvet, its flawless straight lines, its geometrically flexed curves. Vlaminck loves roads: he has followed them at the steering wheel of his automobiles which he has always been driving at breakneck speed. "The sharp turn," says Vlaminck, "that is the place where we should play with that new divinity, the road."

"There are two ways of taking a sharp turn," he says to his daughter Edwige. "Either you slow down and resume speed only after you are well into the turn; or you attack it at 80 miles per hour, brake sharply, skid on your rear wheels, and straighten out keeping your foot on the gas."

"That's a fine way to drive," says Edwige. "It's a way to kill oneself."

"It's my way," Vlaminck says phlegmatically.

Painted 1955

THE BOISSY-MAUGIS ROAD IN LE PERCHE

23⅜ x 28¾"

One of Vlaminck's Flemish inheritances is a kind of affection for snow, even though he knows how cruel snow can be. He saw it blanket the plain in the distance, from Mons to Tournai. Against such snow Bruegel silhouetted bare trees and tiny human figures, all wrapped up and shivering; Vlaminck has obtained magnificent effects with it. The site shown here evokes many memories in him, some of these fairly recent, for in 1940 the Boissy-Maugis road was snowbound, and all the surrounding region was cut off. The inhabitants had to live as they had lived at the time of Bruegel; they had to grind wheat with makeshift tools, and bake their bread at home. Vlaminck's snow is not a literary phenomenon. The Dutch and the Belgians often say that only one modern painter knows what snow, real snow, is — Vlaminck.

Painted 1955

ARCOTTE, ON THE ORLEANS ROAD

23⅜ x 28¾"

The poetry of the road, in which the truck driver has replaced the carter, and in which the horse is unknown, haunts Vlaminck.

The road has secrets of its own; sometimes its face is frightening. Vlaminck shows it to us here as it enters a village which it traverses like a projectile, glistening, slippery, reflecting the frozen fire of neon lights. The dangers of the road excite Vlaminck instead of making him careful. A former mechanic at the Spad works, he finds it hard to keep from stepping on the gas.

His driving license dates from 1920. The first car he owned was an eight-cylinder Ballot. Then he had a powerful American car, which was later succeeded by others. Vlaminck says that he never had an accident. And this is true. But he always touches wood when he says it.

Plate 37. HOUSE AMONG TREES. *Woodcut*

Plate 38. VILLAGE LE PERCHE. *1935. Etching and engraving*
Bibliothèque nationale

BIOGRAPHICAL NOTES

1876   Maurice de Vlaminck, son of Edmond Julien de
Vlaminck and of Julien's wife, née Grillet, is
born in Paris, Rue Pierre-Lescot, on April 4, 1876.

1879   Moves with family to Le Vésinet near Paris.

1896   At twenty takes part in the first Paris-Bordeaux
bicycle race. Successful in a number of sports
events; classified "professional" cyclist and oars-
man. Married and father of three children —
Madeleine, Solange, and Yolande.

1897   Called to the colors, serves as infantryman at
Vitré. Member of the regimental band; plays the
bass drum during marches and the violin at
"concerts in town".

1900   Plays the violin at the Petit Casino and in the
Marchetti Orchestra during the World's Fair of
1900, as well as at the Château d'Eau theater.

Plate 39. ENVIRONS OF PONTOISE. *1925. Lithograph*

1900   Has to work to support himself, and paints during his rare leisure moments. Meets Derain at Pont de Chatou, in the former Le Vanneur restaurant, adjoining the café of Père Fournaise where Renoir painted his *Canotiers*.

1901   Discovers the painting of Van Gogh. Supports himself and his family by playing the violin in various orchestras and beer gardens, and by teaching music.

1905   Discovers the painting of Cézanne.

1905   Exhibits at the Independents, then at the Salon d'Automne, at the same time as Derain and Matisse.

1906   Vollard visits his studio and buys all his paintings.

1907   Still considers the violin his safest means of support, but now gives up all other activities, confining himself to violin playing and painting.

1907   This year marks the beginning of his gradual estrangement from Derain, who moves to the Rue Bonaparte.

1910   Kahnweiler, the art dealer, in agreement with Vollard, concludes a contract with him. He paints continually at Chatou, Rueil, and Bougival.

1911   Supports himself and his family entirely by proceeds from his paintings.

1914   Early that year, viewing Cubist paintings at Paul Guillaume's, has a kind of premonition. "Suddenly I had a glimpse of the coming war," he says.

1914   At age of 38 drafted in the reserves.

1916   Put to work in a munitions factory. Has a brother employed at the Spad airplane works at La Courneuve.

1917   Rents a studio in Paris, 26, Rue du Départ.

1918   Several galleries (Vildrac's and those owned by the Bernheims Jeune) agree to take everything he paints.

1920   Leaves the Rue du Départ and moves to Auvers-Valmondois where his daughter Edwige is born.

1925   Leaves Valmondois and buys the farmhouse called La Tourillière at Beauce in the commune of Rueil-la-Gadelière.

1927   Birth of his daughter Godelieve at La Tourillière.

1930   Without breaking off with Vildrac and the Bernheims he frees himself from contractual obligations toward them.

1955   Since 1925, except for short trips to Brittany, southern France, and his native region, Vlaminck has been living an active life at La Tourillière. In his triple capacity as farmer, writer, and painter, he is one of the most dynamic and most "topical" figures of our time.

Plate 40. VILLAGE STREET. *Drawing*

BIBLIOGRAPHY

I. — *Monographs:*

DANIEL HENRY. *Maurice de Vlaminck.* Leipzig, 1920.

GEORGES DUHAMEL. *Maurice de Vlaminck.* Paris, Ed. les Ecrivains réunis, 1927.

FLORENT FELS. *Vlaminck.* Paris, Ed. Marcel Seneur, 1928.

ANDRÉ MANTAIGNE. *Maurice de Vlaminck.* Paris, Ed. Crès, 1929.

PIERRE MAC-ORLAN (Introduction by). *Vlaminck, peintures 1900—1945.* Paris. Ed. du Chêne, 1947.

MAURICE GENEVOIX. *Vlaminck, l'Homme, l'Œuvre* (120 reprod.) Paris, Flammarion, 1954.

II. — *Chapters or essays in Works on Modern Painting:*

JACQUES GUENNE. *Portraits d'Artistes.* Paris, Ed. Marcel Seneur, 1927. pp. 265—290.

R. HUYGHE and G. BAZIN. *Les Contemporains.* Paris, Ed. Tisné, 1939.

BERNARD DORIVAL. *Les étapes de la Peinture française contemporaine.* Paris, Gallimard, 1944. II, pp. 141—153.

M. RAYNAL. *Histoire de la peinture contemporaine (de Matisse à Rouault).* Geneva, Skira, 1950. p. 62 and p. 146.

III. — *Principal Articles in Periodicals:*

ANDRÉ SALMON. "Vlaminck" in *L'Art vivant,* 1920, pp. 93—98.

Maandblad voor beeldende Kunsten, 1925, No. 2, pp. 130—138.

JEAN CASSOU. "M. de Vlaminck" in *Art et Décoration,* 1929, pp. 65—75.

Dedalo, 1933, No. 13, pp. 175—191.

R. HUYGHE and G. BAZIN. "M. de Vlaminck" in *Amour de l'Art,* 1933, No. 6, pp. 129—132.

PRINTED IN HOLLAND
OFFSET SMEETS WEERT